The Cat Maintenance Manual

Grace McHattie

The Cat Maintenance Manual

200 TIPS FOR OWNERS

With illustrations by John Mansbridge

Methuen · London

First published in Great Britain 1985
by Methuen London Ltd
11 New Fetter Lane, London EC4P 4EE
Text © 1985 Grace McHattie
Illustrations © 1985 John Mansbridge
Reproduced, printed and bound in Great Britain by
Hazell Watson & Viney Limited,
Member of the BPCC Group,
Aylesbury, Bucks

British Library Cataloguing in Publication Data

McHattie, Grace
   The cat maintenance manual: 200 tips for owners.
   1. Cats
   I. Title
   636.8'083   SF447

   ISBN 0 413 59580 3

*To Morgan, Merlin
and Indiana Pudding*

Contents

Preface

There are hundreds of cat *care* manuals on the
market. This isn't one of them.

This book is planned for the ordinary cat-owner who
might benefit from a few tips, hints and warnings that
can't be found put together anywhere else. They
should make life a little easier for the cat-owner and a
little more comfortable for the cat.

For the sake of convenience, I have referred to cats as
'he' unless specifically talking about females. This
should certainly not be taken to imply that male cats
are in any way superior to females.

I hope that there is something useful here for all who
share their lives with that most complex and fascinat-
ing of creatures – the domestic cat.

The early days

When your kitten (or cat) first comes to live with you, give him a temporary name, just to be going on with. You'll try at least three or four names before you find one which suits both of you – and to which he'll answer!

The best place to buy a kitten is from a friend whose cat has had a litter – that way you'll know the temperament of at least one parent.

If your friends' cats don't oblige, take a look at the notice-board in your local veterinary surgery. Kittens and cats are often advertised there and the vet should know the background and health record of the kittens.

When choosing a kitten, from whatever source, check the health signs. The kitten should have clear, bright eyes with no signs of 'weeping'; pink gums (not red); firm white teeth; clean ears with no smell (don't be afraid to sniff!); and a clean, unmatted coat (part the fur; there should be no black specks of flea dirt and no scaly, unhealthy looking skin). Breath should not have a strong smell. Also, have a look under the kitten's tail to ensure there are no traces of diarrhoea.

You can, of course, offer a good home to a kitten which has *not* been properly cared for, but this is not recommended for anyone acquiring their first cat. And always be prepared for heartbreak if the kitten doesn't recover his health.

When choosing a kitten, don't automatically choose the most extrovert, which will come bouncing out of his basket to greet you. He will probably grow into an independent and strong-willed cat, and that may not suit *your* personality. If you're looking for a quiet, friendly companion, the shy kitten which holds back could be the one you should choose.

Kittens shouldn't leave their mothers until they're eight weeks old or more. They can develop behavioural problems in later life if taken away too early.

If offered a pure-white kitten, try to make an unexpected sound (like clicking your fingers) without the kitten noticing the movement required to make it. Some white kittens are deaf or partially deaf, and you may be able to gauge this from their reaction (or lack of it) to the sound. Deaf cats can make charming and intelligent pets, but it would be unfair to expect one to live near a busy road or close to unsympathetic humans or dogs.

If you'd like to buy a pedigree kitten, start looking several months before you want it. There are often waiting lists for good kittens before they're born.

To find a pedigree kitten, visit a cat show and look for a cat which appeals to you. You can ask if she will be having kittens, or if the breeder has similar cats which will be having kittens. The owners of pedigree cats are never far away from them at shows. Don't be afraid to chat to the owner – pedigree cat-owners like nothing better than to talk about their cats.

Or, you can find a list of pedigree cat-breeders in a cat magazine. Contact one of them – but don't feel you

have to buy the first kitten you're shown. No reputable breeder will be offended if you don't like a cat's
temperament or colour. They want to find good
homes for their kittens – which means matching
owner and kitten exactly.

Remember to tell the breeder if you want a 'pet'
quality kitten. 'Show' quality kittens have no better
temperament and won't look much different to the
non-expert, but may cost four or five times as much
as a 'pet'.

Before bringing a new kitten home, make sure you
know where your nearest veterinary surgery is. You
never know when you'll need a vet in an emergency,
and hunting through the telephone directory in a
panic is never a good idea. Talk to your pet-owning
friends and ask them to recommend a good vet
nearby.

Before booking any non-emergency treatment, such
as neutering, phone several veterinary practices and
ask about their charges. Fees vary according to the
vet's overheads and the cost of neutering a tomcat
can vary by more than £10. Don't, of course, auto-

matically use the cheapest vet. If you can find a less expensive vet who has been recommended by a friend, you're getting the best of both worlds.

There are thousands of unwanted cats in the world, so don't let your cat add to the total. Have females spayed and males neutered at the age recommended by your vet. Some vets like to carry out the operation when the kitten is three months old, while others prefer to wait until six or even eight months.

Remember, don't feed your cat on the day of any operation, including spaying and neutering.

Spaying or neutering your cat is to your benefit too. Entire (unneutered) tomcats mark their territory by spraying their pungent urine anywhere they feel like it, often all over your home. Neutering usually stops this. Neutered tomcats have smaller territories than whole tomcats, so are less likely to stray or get lost. Whole (unspayed) females (also called queens) will attract tomcats from a wide area, who will spray anywhere they can reach!

Females usually come into season (on heat) the first spring after they turn six months of age, although some come into season earlier, especially Siamese and part-Siamese. If you haven't had your cat spayed, be alert for unusual behaviour. She may become excessively friendly, or growl at you, but she will almost certainly roll around and stretch out on the floor. Many owners panic when they first see a cat in season, believing her to be hurt or ill, but she's not in any pain. There may also be a loud 'calling'. Tomcats will congregate outside your door, attracted by her scent over a long distance. Don't bother shooing them – they won't go until the season is over, several days later. If you don't want a litter of kittens, keep your cat indoors. Have her spayed when the season is over, *not* during it, as this can lead to medical complications. Remember, the caterwauling you'll have to live through is your fault, not hers. You should have had her spayed sooner!

To help a new kitten settle down on his first few nights, wrap a warm hot-water bottle in a blanket in his bed. A ticking clock can also be put under the blanket. He'll think he's still with his mum, listening to her heartbeat.

Make sure your kitten becomes used to eating a variety of foods. Cats which are fed on only one food become faddy and, frankly, a nuisance. However, for the first few days he's with you, let him have the food he's used to – it will help him to settle down.

Try to accustom your cat from kittenhood to being locked *in* at night, especially if you live in a town or city. He's more likely to get into fights at night when tomcats are on the prowl and he runs more risk of being stolen during the hours of darkness. Many cats don't mind spending their nights indoors as long as they've been used to it from an early age. Provide a clean litter tray for night-time use.

Young kittens often eat cat litter – no one knows why. To ensure this does them no harm, use a natural product with no additives. Fullers' earth litter is one of the natural mineral clays, crushed and dried, so eating small quantities will cause no problems. It's readily available from pet shops and supermarkets and can be distinguished by its grey colour and heavier weight.

If your kitten becomes quiet and loses his normal healthy appetite, he could be suffering from worms. A fat, tight tummy is another sign and the kitten may vomit or have occasional diarrhoea. If you're in *any* doubt about what is ailing your kitten, consult your vet immediately.

Kittens and adult cats should be wormed regularly to control roundworms. Palatable wormers can be crushed and added to food and are sold in all pet shops. Check the packet for frequency of treatment.

If you notice small specks like grains of rice around your cat's bottom, this could be a symptom of tapeworms. Your vet can supply the most effective worming tablets. Roundworm tablets are ineffective against tapeworms.

Always ask your vet's advice about worming very young kittens. Dosage is critical in the early months and the wrong drug or an overdose could be fatal.

Speak to your vet about vaccinations – vets have their own ideas about when the first one should be given; it can be as early as eight weeks. Cats can be given a triple vaccine for *Feline Panleucopenia/Feline Viral Rhinotracheitis/Feline Calici Virus.* A second dose is given three to six weeks after the first dose, then boosters are given once a year.

Many people don't have their cats vaccinated. Apart from running the risk of their cat catching a fatal disease, no reputable boarding cattery will accept a cat which has not been vaccinated and no cat can enter a licensed cat show without an up-to-date vaccination certificate.

If your cat is to have kittens, place several kittening boxes (cardboard boxes with 8-inch or 10-inch walls will do) in quiet, convenient positions around the house. When the time comes, your cat will probably choose one of them. If she doesn't, place a box in the place *she*'s chosen. Don't try to change her mind; she'll keep returning to her choice of nursery, carrying her kittens with her.

Line her box with a warm blanket and place plenty of sheets of white kitchen paper or white tissue paper on top. As they get soiled, they can be removed, a sheet at a time, with the minimum disturbance to the new family. It's easy to see when the paper becomes dirty, and white paper contains no dyes to irritate young skin.

Prohibit visitors for the first few weeks. Mum will want peace and quiet. If she doesn't get it, she may try to hide her kittens somewhere.

You'll want to check over very young kittens regularly to ensure they're healthy. This can be diffi-cult single-handed as they squirm and wriggle con-tinuously. Mum stops them wriggling by picking them up by the scruff of the neck – they immediately go limp. You can copy this idea but leave both hands free. Hold the kitten in the proper manner (one hand under bottom, other hand supporting chest) but briefly clamp a wooden clothespeg onto the skin at the back of his neck. The peg will stop him wriggling, but make sure it doesn't grip too tightly, and don't, of course, use the peg to pick him up.

Never pick kittens up by the scruff of the neck as this puts undue strain on their neck muscles. Their mother picks them up that way – but she doesn't have the alternative of hands.

Never advertise kittens as 'free to a good home'. Putting a price on them (which, ultimately, you need not charge) means that there is more likelihood of them becoming treasured pets. Don't rely on that alone – tell any enquirers that you'd like to see the facilities they'll provide for the kitten and visit their home. If they're hesitant, don't part with the kitten. People really do answer 'free kitten' ads, taking their families, including young children, along to persuade owners that they want a pet. Then they sell the kittens to laboratories or to fur dealers, for pelts.

Cats can be trained to behave in a way that enables them to live in harmony with their owners, but training should begin young. A firm 'no' and removal from whatever they're doing is often enough to get the idea across. If you want to get really heavy, the firm 'no' coupled with a gentle shake should do it. Don't slap a naughty cat – you'll end up with a nervous, naughty cat.

Never buy a kitten at Christmas. There's too much noise and disruption at that time for a young animal to settle down. If a child insists on having a kitten for Christmas, buy a toy one, explaining that the real thing will arrive once the house is back to normal.

Introductions

When meeting a cat for the first time, get down on your hands and knees. If you tower over a cat, he'll take it as a threat. Talk quietly to him and don't extend your hand until he's accepted your company.

Never tickle a cat's tum until invited to do so – a cat's stomach is a very vulnerable part of his body and he will only expose it to someone he feels secure with. Tickling, before being invited to do so, is considered over-familiar.

Let a cat explore his new home at his own pace. It's best to keep him in one room at first. He'll want to find a hiding-place – see page 36 for tips on a *convenient* hiding-place.

Introducing a new cat or kitten into a household where there already is a cat may produce problems.

The senior cat can feel that his territory is being threatened, and cats *can* feel insecure, which may lead to all sorts of behavioural problems. So:

Before you make friends with the newcomer, let him make friends with your senior cat. Cats are sensitive creatures and may never forgive you if you make too much fuss of a newcomer.

Blunt both cats' claws using nail clippers or claw clippers, which you can buy from most pet shops. Take off only the very tip (see page 29). If the cats do fight, they'll do one another less harm with blunt claws.

Cats rely heavily on their sense of smell and won't like the newcomer, who will smell strangely of other places. You can make them smell the same by wiping their coats with a solution of one tablespoon of cider vinegar in two pints of water. Saturate their coats – but *not* around their eyes (or other openings) or over cuts or scratches. When dry, they should accept one another's smells more happily.

If this is not enough, baby powder can be rubbed into their coats and the excess brushed out. Be careful they don't inhale any powder and don't get any in their eyes.

If one of the cats is being particularly difficult, use a cat-breeders' trick. Place the newcomer in a large pen for a few days where he can see and be seen but not got at. (Don't forget to give him a litter tray, food and water.) Let him out at feeding time, when your senior cat has his mind on other things. If they persist in fighting, put the newcomer back in the pen for a day or two. It sounds drastic but it's better than having his eyes scratched out!

Play sessions with both cats involved helps them to settle down together. If they're busy attacking a piece of string trailed by you or chasing a ball, they're too busy to annoy one another.

Health

Out-of-condition cats can become nervous, listless and disinterested in their surroundings. They may lose their appetites and their skin can become scaly with some fur loss. Conditioning tablets for cats are readily available in pet shops. Follow dosage instructions carefully. Or add cod-liver oil to their food. It's as good for cats as it is for children. A pinch of wheat-germ added to food can also help.

Vitamin E can benefit cats too. It can be purchased from a chemist, pet shop or herbalist and added to food. You can also use it to clean a cat's ears by dampening cotton-wool swabs with vitamin E oil. Some will be absorbed through the skin and grooming will distribute more.

Always ensure when cleaning a cat's ears that the swab is kept parallel to the ear. The ear can be damaged if the swab is inserted too far into the ear or pushed too hard against the sides.

Cover a pill or tablet with cream cheese and you'll find that your cat will gobble it up. He'll love the cheese and it's so sticky, he can't spit it out.

Fur balls can be a problem, especially in a long-haired cat, as some fur is always swallowed when the cat grooms himself. This can collect in the intestines if the cat is unable to pass it. So brush or comb the cat regularly. An occasional dose of medicinal liquid paraffin or oil from a tin of tuna or sardines will help him to eliminate fur balls from his body. Or smear some petroleum jelly on his paws occasionally. He'll lick it off and it will serve the same purpose.

Both medicinal liquid paraffin and petroleum jelly also help with constipation.

A convalescent cat often refuses solid food. Try him with his favourite food liquidised with a little milk, water or stock, which he can – and will – lap up.

If your cat has been ill or is recovering from kittening, an invalid food for humans will help build her up again. Use the unflavoured variety and mix in a stock cube for added interest.

Often, sick cats can't smell their food so they'll ignore it. Try feeding them strong-smelling food such as sardines or adding meat or yeast extract to their usual meat or fish.

To feed an ill cat with liquids, buy a syringe from a chemist (they are very cheap) and throw away the needle. Fill the syringe with liquid and release gently between the lips into the side of your cat's mouth. (Do not push the syringe down his throat.) This is a good way to give liquid medicine too. You'll have better control over the amount fed and will be able to gauge this exactly because of the measurements on the side of the syringe.

Make sure you have a proper carrying basket for trips in the car or to the vet. So that your cat won't associate it only with unpleasant things like inoculations, leave it in an accessible place where your cat can play in it between trips.

Combination carrying baskets/beds are available, so it can serve two purposes.

If you're travelling to the vet with a sick or incontinent cat, line his basket with a baby's disposable nappy. It can be easily and conveniently replaced if it becomes soiled.

Some elderly and incontinent cats can even be persuaded to *wear* a disposable nappy – with a hole cut out for his tail to come through, of course.

If you have to restrain a cat, wrap a towel around him so that his body is covered but his head is free. Hold the towel around him at the neck. Remember to talk quietly and reassuringly to him before, during and after restraint.

Don't let a shortage of cash deprive your pet of necessary veterinary treatment. The People's Dispensary for Sick Animals (PDSA) runs more than 70 clinics throughout the country where any pet will be treated free if the owner can't afford to pay.

If your cat is seriously ill, he should, of course, be receiving veterinary treatment. If a very ill cat begins to purr, this is a warning signal and you should contact your vet immediately. Cats purr, not only in great joy, but when they're in great pain.

Food and drink

It's important for a cat's health that he drinks plenty
of liquids – especially if dry food is given. If your cat
won't drink plain tap water, try him with cooled
boiled water. Or try adding a little honey to the water.
Some cats prefer rainwater, but be careful it isn't
polluted. Or bottle water for a day or two before
pouring it into your cat's bowl. The chlorinated smell,
which is often off-putting to cats, will have dispersed.
If all else fails, make up a 'soup' from giblets or bones.
Strain and allow to cool. Pour the liquid into your
cat's bowl and stand back!

Cats don't *need* milk if their diet is good. It's an
unnatural food for any mammal, once weaned. But if
you'd like your cat to drink milk and he won't, trying
using reconstituted dried milk. Cats often prefer it.
This is worth trying, too, for a cat which suffers from
diarrhoea with ordinary milk. The problem may clear
up when you switch to dried milk.

Ideally, water bowls should be kept in a different
room from food bowls. In the wild, cats never eat
near their waterhole.

If you are away from home with your cat for a few
hours or a few days, take a supply of drinking water
with you. Water varies throughout the country and a
cat will be happier with water he is used to.

Cats hate to eat from dirty feeding bowls – just like us. If you find washing-up a chore, use paper plates and dispose of them after one use. They're hygienic and fairly cheap if you buy them in bulk.

Some cats are sensitive to polythene or plastic. If your cat reacts to it, possibly with a skin rash, ceramic or stainless steel feeding bowls will have to be used. Food should be stored in glass or ceramic containers.

Keep a spoon and tin-opener specially for your cat's tinned food. It's possible to contract food poisoning from using cutlery which has come into contact with a cat's food.

For a fussy eater, a tiny pinch of catnip (also called catmint) sprinkled over the cat's food can encourage him to eat. You can buy catnip from a herbalist or health food shop, or grow your own from seed.

If your cat trails his food onto the floor or even tries picking it up with his paws, his feeding bowl may be too narrow. Cats don't like eating from a dish which is narrower than their whiskers. Or perhaps he doesn't like the smell of washing-up liquid. Give his bowl a final rinse in a solution of baking soda and water to eradicate all smells.

When a tin of food is finished, flatten the tin with a hammer. Otherwise, a foraging cat can cut himself while trying to lick the inside of the tin, or may even get his head stuck. The tin will take up less space in the dustbin too.

If you find money-off offers on dry cat food, buy as much as you can and store it in tightly sealed containers until you're ready to use it. You can mix different flavours too. It should keep for up to a year.

For a supper snack, or as part of a late meal, provide your cat with some dry cat food. It not only helps to exercise his jaws, it also helps to prevent the formation of tartar on the teeth. Even cats should clean their teeth before bed!

Cats dislike cold food straight from the fridge. So, if you buy the largest cans for economy, divide the contents into meal-sized portions and put them in lidded food-storage containers. Keep them in the fridge until about an hour before meal-times, when they can be taken out to warm up. Or warm them quickly by placing them in a basin of hot water. These containers can also be used to freeze meal-size portions. Remove from the freezer several hours before use.

For economy, you can bulk out your cat's food by using up to one-third cooked potato mixed with his regular tinned or dry food or fish. Or feed one-third boiled rice mixed with two-thirds meat or fish. Or add a little wholemeal bread or vegetables to meat or fish.

If you change your cat's food, do it gradually. A sudden change from one brand of food to another will almost always cause diarrhoea.

To change a fussy cat's diet, start adding the new food to his old food in small amounts and mix thoroughly. Increase the amount each day until he's eating the food you want him to eat.

You'll never find a finicky eater in a household with more than one cat. The fusspot soon finds that if he doesn't eat as soon as the food hits the plate, someone else will eat it for him. If buying another cat is an over-drastic solution to the fussy eater, emulate the multi-cat situation. After ten minutes, remove the food bowl and don't replace it until the next meal-time. This *will* work, but you'll need to develop a heart of stone.

In the wild, a cat will kill his prey and eat his fill, then may not eat for two or three days. Bear this in mind next time your cat makes it plain that he'll starve before he eats the food in his bowl because he prefers another flavour! Leave it until he does eat it (unless it goes off first, which is highly unlikely, or unless it has attracted flies).

Raw meat (including some fat) is ideal for cats nutritionally, but can contain parasites if sold as unfit for human consumption. Always cook this type of meat. Meat fit for human consumption can be served raw and raw mince is a great treat.

Don't feed your cat exclusively on fish – it isn't a natural food for a feline. In the wild, he'd eat a combination of rodents, birds and insects – but he'll probably settle for a well-balanced tinned food.

To cook your cat's fish economically and without smell, place it in a saucepan and cover with boiling water. Replace the lid and leave for 10 minutes without further heating. The fish will cook without any additional use of fuel and your home will remain fragrant!

If you would like to give your cat a nutritious treat, spread some thinly-cut wholemeal bread with marmite. Cut into 1-inch squares and stand back before you lose your fingers!

If you suspect that your cat is being fed by a neighbour and is consequently gaining weight, feed him less attractive food. Most cats aren't crazy about tinned mackerel or pilchards, so will only eat them if genuinely hungry. (Always ensure that a fat cat isn't displaying one of the symptoms of worms – check with your vet if in doubt.)

If you share your home with another person, your cat will become a master at letting you know that your house-mate has forgotten to feed him. Then *you* will feed him, only to discover later that your cat deserves an Oscar for his acting. Hang a piece of cardboard from a hook near your cat's feeding-place. One side of the cardboard should read 'cat fed – morning' and the reverse should read 'cat fed – evening'. Whoever feeds the cat turns the cardboard round, so the other person knows it's been done. Otherwise, you could end up with a very happy but fat cat!

It isn't a good idea to feed your cat on demand – he'll simply demand food more often! Twice a day, morning and evening, is often enough and your cat will quickly adjust to your schedule.

If giving tinned or dry food, feed the amount recommended on the tin or packet. If your cat seems genuinely hungry and looks thin on the recommended amounts, increase until he seems satisfied. As a general rule, adult males should weigh $7\frac{1}{2}$ to 11 lbs ($3\frac{1}{2}$ to 5 kgs) and adult females $5\frac{1}{2}$ to 8 lbs ($2\frac{1}{2}$ to 3 kgs).

Adult cats require *approximately* 350 calories a day, but this varies according to age, activity and other factors. If you feed fatty foods, such as minced beef, four tablespoons a day will provide 350 calories, but eight tablespoons will have to be fed of less fatty food such as white fish.

If you like your cat to go outdoors to relieve himself, you can save your energy by installing a cat-flap in an outside door. Unfortunately, everyone else's cat will use it too, so make sure it has a lock. With one make of cat-flap, a locking plate has to be purchased separately, but this is an essential piece of equipment.

There are two types of cat-flap which will open selectively. Both necessitate the cat wearing a collar which will activate the flap. One works electro-magnetically, so any cat with a magnetic collar will gain access. There is also an electronic, battery-operated cat-flap opened by the approach of a cat wearing a collar complete with transmitter tuned to that particular frequency. Both flaps currently cost around £35.

When installing a cat-flap, always ensure that it is positioned further than arm's-length from the door lock. Otherwise, it's possible for a burglar to reach through and unlock the door.

If your cat is hesitant about using his new flap, leave it propped open at first. When he's used to it, close it when he's outside and prepare his meal. Most cats will learn instantly how to get through a cat-flap when there is food on the other side!

If your cat uses cat litter, it is more economic to fill the tray to a depth of two or three inches, especially if the very absorbent Fullers' earth is used. Liquid waste will saturate a shallow amount of litter, but will form a small wet ball in several inches of litter. The wet ball is easily lifted out with a scoop or spoon, leaving the remaining litter clean. Your cat can more easily bury solid waste in deeper litter, so there will be no smell.

Litter lasts longer if you use several sheets of newspaper to line the tray. Pull out the top, wet layer of paper each day, leaving behind the dry, fresh litter.

Cut down a large cardboard box so that the sides are 6 to 8 inches high. Place your cat's litter tray inside this. It will stop litter scattering over your floor and you can tip the saved litter back into the tray.

Keep your litter box sitting inside a clean, empty one. If you're pushed for time, you can simply put the used tray outside for cleaning later. In the meantime, fill the replacement tray.

If you need to take a sample of your cat's urine to the vet, shred unused kitchen paper into a clean litter tray. When your cat has used it, squeeze out the liquid into a container.

When house-training a young kitten, place him on his litter tray an hour or so after every meal.

A little catnip sprinkled in the litter tray is often an incentive for cats who are reluctant to use it.

Some kittens, once trained to use a litter tray, will insist on coming indoors to use it. If you want to break this habit, place the tray a little nearer the door each day, until, eventually, the tray is outside. Or, sprinkle a little soil (preferably sterilised soil or potting compost) on top of the litter as a hint.

Some cats will scratch *outside* their tray when 'covering up'. This can lead to confusion in the cat's mind. He may start to use the carpet as a lavatory if this is what he's felt under his paws when covering up. The simple solution is to place the tray on a large sheet of plastic, or inside a cardboard box.

If a cat of previously clean habits starts relieving himself somewhere he shouldn't, seek veterinary advice immediately – this could be the first symptom of an illness.

If your cat chooses one particular spot to relieve himself, place a clean litter tray there – even if it *is* in the middle of the living-room. Once the cat gets used to using the tray, it can be moved, a short space at a time, to a more convenient position.

If your cat relieves himself somewhere you simply can't place a litter tray, place a chair or other obstacle there. Make sure you clean the area thoroughly first so that there are no lingering smells to remind your cat that this was once his loo.

A cat may refuse to use his litter tray for many reasons. He may not like the smell of whatever you use to clean it. Or you may be using a cleanser which is toxic to cats (see page 41). Try a different cleanser. Or add baking soda to the final rinse water. It will neutralise smells. Some cats are repelled by the smell of urine. Baking soda will help there too.

If that fails, try a different type of litter. Some cats prefer one type of litter over another, or may even be allergic to some types.

Some cats, most particularly some long-hairs, don't like getting litter on their fur. Try using shredded kitchen paper instead. Or use dry sand. Or dry peat – although you may end up with black footprints all over the house!

If you have more than one cat, you may have to provide individual litter trays. Some cats won't use a tray another cat has used.

If possible, keep the litter tray in another room from the one in which your cat is fed. Cats prefer not to eat in the bathroom!

Some cats require privacy. If there isn't a quiet cubby-hole somewhere where you can place his tray, try using one of the new-design covered litter trays. The cat can climb right inside this type of tray.

Keep a bowl of pot-pourri in the room where your cat's litter tray stands. Any temporary odours from the tray will be masked by flower scent.

Grooming

Although cats are very clean animals, they will benefit from an occasional beauty treatment. You can buy dry shampoos specially formulated for cats from a pet shop or you can use talcum powder or cornflour on a pale-coloured cat. Finely crushed Fullers' earth makes a good dry shampoo for a brown or red cat. Make sure your cat doesn't swallow or inhale any powder. Brush until all the powder has gone.

Buy bran from a health food shop or supermarket and give a dark cat a 'bran bath'. Warm a cupful of bran in the oven, making sure it doesn't become hot or it will burn your cat. Rub handfuls into the fur and brush out thoroughly.

It's sometimes necessary to bath a cat, and many don't take kindly to the idea. So one person can place the cat in a sturdy old pillowcase held up around the neck. Cat and bag are placed in a sink with a few inches of warm water in it and a helper washes the cat *through* the bag, using a special cat shampoo or baby shampoo. The cat won't like it any better that way but the pillowcase will stop him making his objections felt!

Always towel-dry your cat as quickly as possible after a bath and ensure that he's kept warm until he's thoroughly dry.

Your cat should be brushed regularly, otherwise he could end up with problems from fur balls. He can't reach every part of himself when grooming, and brushing will also enable you to check for fleas and other parasites. If your cat doesn't like being groomed, persevere. Try brushing him when he's sleeping or dozing on your lap – cats often enjoy grooming then. Or groom him when you come home after a short absence – he'll probably be so pleased to see you that he'll let you do what you like.

When grooming a kitten for the first time, make sure he remembers it as a pleasurable experience. Don't actually brush him for the first few times – just stroke your hands over him as if they were brushes. After a few days, repeat the movements with a brush.

As soon as your cat lets you know he's had enough grooming – stop. Always start and finish with the places your cat really enjoys being groomed – head, neck, chest – he'll soon let you know his favourite areas!

If your cat is elderly, it won't be easy for him to groom but it's still important. Be a pal and brush him daily.

It's been known for some cats to enjoy being vacuum-cleaned! It'll remove loose hair and debris but, obviously, don't try it on a cat who hates the sound of the vacuum-cleaner. And keep it on its lowest setting!

If your cat is too lazy to groom himself, smear fish paste over his fur. He'll lick it off and, with luck, get into the habit.

To make your cat's coat shine after grooming, finish off by stroking his fur with a piece of chamois or silk wrapped around your hand.

If your cat has been walking on a newly tarred road, don't allow him to try licking off the tar. Instead, scrape off as much as possible using the blunt edge of a table knife and then rub butter on the paws and wipe with cotton wool. For tar on the coat, rub with cool melted butter and wipe off.

For a cheap cat brush, use a doll's hairbrush or an old baby brush – bristle is best.

Dandruff combs meant for human heads are cheaper than flea combs. Be sure to check that there are no sharp edges to scratch your cat's skin.

Never trim your cat's claws too short. They will bleed copiously if you do. Consult a good cat care book or ask your vet if you need to learn how to do it.

Cats not only enjoy clawing – they *need* to do it. It exercises their muscles, cleans off the old, shredded portion of their claws and is another way in which they mark their territory. If you don't supply your cat with a suitable scratching post, he'll use your best furniture – and it serves you right! You can make an inexpensive scratching post easily, but make sure it's at least 30 inches high. Your cat needs to stretch.

If you have an old kitchen table with wooden legs, nail one end of a thin rope about 30 inches from the base. Then wind the rope round and round the leg, remembering to cover the nail head completely, which should be flush with the wood. Secure at the bottom by placing the remaining end of the rope under the table leg. Another nail can secure it in place.

Nail a leftover piece of strong carpeting to a wall or the side of a kitchen unit. Make sure that the nails are above the height of the cat at full stretch and that they don't protrude.

Nail strong corrugated cardboard to a wall or kitchen unit. Cats enjoy scratching it and it's easily and cheaply replaced.

A piece of driftwood found on a beach or an interestingly shaped piece of tree-trunk brought home and thoroughly washed makes a great scratching post and may even enhance your decor!

Your cat may not use whatever scratching post you provide at first. After all, you spend most of your time telling him *not* to scratch. So demonstrate. Get down on your knees and scratch the post with long, sweeping motions of your hands. Your cat will look at you as if you've gone crazy but he'll get the idea.

If he doesn't, rub catnip on the post. Many cats love the smell and will soon associate it with things they're allowed to scratch.

If your cat won't stop scratching a particular piece of furniture, cover it with a large sheet of plastic. Cats hate the feel of plastic and will give it a miss. After a few weeks, you can remove the plastic and hope he's forgotten that it used to be a fun scratchpad.

Fleas

Now that many homes have wall-to-wall carpeting and central heating, cat fleas have become more of a problem than ever before, because fleas thrive in comfortable surroundings too. Most cats will acquire some of these passengers at some time in their lives and there's nothing shameful about having a cat with fleas – only in having a cat with untreated fleas.

You will know your cat has fleas if you part the fur and see tiny black specks (flea dirt) or red specks of dried blood. Your cat will scratch too.

One of the easiest ways to control fleas is by asking a friend to walk through your house while you're on holiday. Fleas lay their eggs in carpets or rugs. The larvae hatch in response to the vibration of the movement of your cat – and leap aboard for their first meal. So when you go on holiday, arrange for a friend to walk through the house a few days before you come back. The larvae will hatch in response to the movement but, because there is no living creature for them to feed on, they'll starve to death before you get home!

As fleas lay their eggs in carpeting and other soft furnishings, you'll collect some every time you vacuum. However, they can still hatch. If you don't want a bag full of bugs, keep a flea collar in the vacuum bag. (Make sure you take it off the cat first.)

To help eliminate fleas without using chemicals, place a reading lamp on the floor so that the light shines onto a shallow pan of soapy water. Fleas will be attracted to the light and will drown in the water.

Wormwood (*Artemesia Absinthium*) is a perennial herb which you can grow from seed in a pot or in your garden. It yields a bitter oil and dried wormwood leaves can be used as a flea deterrent. Rub them into your cat's coat, then brush out thoroughly. Place some wormwood in a cloth bag in your cat's bed and it will repel fleas there too.

Garlic, given internally in the form of capsules or chopped fresh garlic added to a cat's food, has the reputation as a flea repellant. Well, it repels most things!

If you have to trim a flea collar before it fits your cat, don't throw away the remaining piece. Put it near your cat's favourite sleeping place, where it can continue working.

When flea collars lose their efficiency, don't throw them away. Keep them as replacement straps for cat-carrying baskets.

If your cat hates the sound of the flea spray, buy it in liquid or powder form. Put it in a hair-tinting bottle – the type with a long nozzle. Make partings 1 inch apart in your cat's fur and spread the liquid or powder along the skin. Rub in and after a few minutes, brush out thoroughly.

Never use a flea spray on your cat within several days of worming him. Used together, the two treatments can be toxic.

Holidays and moving

Some owners take their cats on holiday with them.
Cats are fiercely territorial animals and many react
very badly to having their territory changed. Don't
take your cat away with you unless you are certain he
will settle down very quickly. Most cats won't.

Never take your cat abroad on holiday with you.
Because of rabies laws, you will have to quarantine
your cat for six months on your return to Britain.

Never consider smuggling your cat into Britain from
abroad. Apart from the possibility of introducing the
deadly and horrifying disease of rabies, if you're
caught, you'll face an unlimited fine or up to a year's
imprisonment. In addition, your cat may be destroyed.

Book your cat's holiday when booking your own.
Most good catteries are fully booked for the summer
by January.

Contact the Feline Advisory Bureau for a list of
approved catteries which fulfil their very high
standards of construction and management. If using a
cattery not on the list, you *must* check it out per-
sonally before booking. If the owner is unwilling to
let you see *all over* the premises, go elsewhere.
Sometimes inferior accommodation is kept out of
sight while you may be shown the 'show homes'. The
owners of well-run catteries will expect you to inspect
their premises thoroughly.

When checking out a cattery, look for cleanliness of litter trays, feeding bowls and runs – there should be no unpleasant smells. Cats should be housed individually, ideally with an impermeable 'sneeze barrier' to minimise the risk of cross-infection between each pen or run.

Cattery owners should appear to care about their charges and the boarders should look contented. Cat runs should have inner and outer doors as many cats try to escape from their confinement.

Tell the cattery owner about your cat's likes and dislikes and take his blanket and a favourite toy so that he feels more at home.

Remember, good cattery owners will insist that your cat is vaccinated before they will agree to take him.

Because of their territorial nature, moving house can be a traumatic time for you *and* your cat. Some cats will be happier if they've been introduced to the new home in small doses. If the new home is empty, take your cat over there a few times, if possible, and let him explore.

On moving day, leave your cat in a room where he won't be disturbed by the removal men – perhaps the bathroom. Leave some toys in there, a litter tray and his bed, then lock the door. When the chaos has subsided, put him into his carrying basket, ready for the move.

At your new home, have a room ready for him where he can remain undisturbed while the removal men *unpack*. Provide him with a hiding-place in the room – he'll be feeling insecure.

A large cardboard box makes a great hiding-place. Tape the lid shut and cut a cat-sized hole in one side, several inches off the ground. Place some dry cat food and/or some catnip in there so that it's a nice place to be. If you think that's a lot of bother, it's much less trouble than coaxing an insecure cat out from under the bath!

When everything has quietened down and the removal men have gone, ensure that all doors and windows are closed, then open the door to your cat's room. Let him come out in his own time and explore at his own pace.

He'll appreciate a few hidey-holes throughout the house until he's feeling more secure, so it's out with the sellotape and scissors again.

Make sure *unsuitable* hiding-places are blocked off completely. Otherwise your cat may spend the first few days in his new home up the chimney!

You can make the transition easier for him if you place the furniture in the same way as at your previous home. You can shift it, piece by piece, when he's settled down.

Have his feeding bowls and litter tray placed in the same way as before. Have a tempting meal and a drink ready for him but don't worry if he's off his food for a day or two.

Don't feed him before you move – it's never a good idea to feed a cat just before a journey. They're often bad travellers and can be sick.

Some people go to the lengths of taking some soiled litter to the new home. The theory is that it's a familiar smell for your cat in unfamiliar surroundings, and helps to mark his territory. Of course, it's probably a familiar smell *you* could do without!

Don't let your cat out for at least a week. He may become confused and try to go back to his old home. Don't worry if your cat shows no inclination to go out for a *month* – it can take a very territorial cat that long to settle down.

When you let your cat out for the first few times, make it a short outing – and go with him. He'll be glad of your company in unfamiliar surroundings. Stay with him for five or ten minutes, then call him in with you when you go. He'll probably be glad of the excuse to go indoors but won't want to lose face by suggesting it himself.

If you're moving to an old property, check if it has been treated for woodworm recently. Some woodworm treatments can be toxic to cats several months after treatment, even when the floors are carpeted afterwards. If you're buying a home and have to have the woodworm treated (some building societies insist) try to arrange for this to be done after you've exchanged contracts and before completion. Some vendors will let you do this – at your own risk and expense, of course. As there is usually several weeks between exchange and completion, this gives the toxic effect time to lessen.

Yes, butter on a cat's paws may help to keep him in a new home. It isn't because of the reason once given – that by the time he's licked it off he'll have forgotten about his old home. Cats have much better memories than that. Licking buttery paws will cover them in saliva which is then distributed throughout the new home, giving it a familiar smell to the cat. It's that familiar smell he misses.

At home

When furnishing your home, never buy a loop-pile carpet. Your cat's claws will catch on it and he'll think the entire living-room is one huge scratching post. Loop-pile will become tattered very quickly.

When buying curtains or re-covering chairs, don't use open weaves or rough textures – they're too attractive to a scratch-loving cat.

If your cat will not leave a new fabric alone, washing it may be enough to discourage him. Some fabrics use a 'size' to stiffen them and give them a better finish, which is made from fish-products. It could be this which is attracting your cat. The smell isn't strong enough for us to notice – but your cat certainly will!

You could try repelling your cat from a particular fabric by soaking it in white vinegar or dabbing it with Tabasco sauce. (Try this on a corner first to make sure it won't stain the fabric.) Or use alum – familiar to all nail-biters. Or, after washing, use vinegar, lemon juice or peppermint oil in the final rinse as a deterrent.

If your cat has a scratching post (see page 30), but insists on clawing the furniture, keep a water-pistol handy. Each time he scratches the furniture, spray him with water. He'll hate it but won't connect the 'punishment' with you. Being a clever creature, a cat will soon stop behaving badly if he gets wet every time he does!

If your furniture is receiving unfair wear and tear from your cat, observe him as he walks through the house. Cats choose very definite pathways which they use time after time. If he has to climb over the settee to get to a favourite spot, move the settee.

If your cat is sick or messes on the carpet, after you've picked it up and washed the area, sprinkle baking soda over it. Leave it for a day or two to dry thoroughly, then vacuum it up. The baking soda will remove any lingering smells.

If your cat persists in jumping onto the kitchen work surfaces or other places you don't want him to go, try smearing the surface with something sticky, like treacle. Cats hate having sticky paws, yet treacle will do them no harm.

Since many disinfectants are toxic to cats (see page 45) the best disinfectant to use on feeding bowls and litter trays is a solution of sodium hypochlorite and water. Sodium hypochlorite is readily available in the

form of Domestos. Use $\frac{1}{4}$ ml Domestos made up to 100 ml with water.

This is also the best solution to use when cleaning kitchen floors and worktops. Some cleansers can also be toxic to cats.

For cleaning cat hair from furniture, spray lightly first using a plant spray-mister containing clean water. It will stop the hairs flying around as you collect them.

If your cat digs up your pot plants, you can stop him by hanging a mothball on a low leaf or placing it on the compost. He'll give the plant a wide berth.
Stop him from eating houseplants by dabbing Tabasco sauce on the leaves or sprinkling them with cayenne pepper.

Cats nibble houseplants because they need some green matter as an aid to digestion. Grow a little tub of grass for him to nibble on and he'll probably leave your plants alone.

Some houseplants can poison cats; for example, dieffenbachias and poinsettias. Cacti can cause a problem too. Some cats will eat them and, although not toxic, the prickles will stick in their throats, requiring veterinary attention.

There are many uses around the home for the heavy, grey type of cat litter – Fullers' earth.
  * An open container of this litter, kept in a wardrobe, will help to absorb moisture and stop clothes mildewing if the air is damp.
  * A cupful in a fridge will absorb smells.
  * A few handfuls in front of your car's wheels will help them grip if you're stuck in ice or snow.

* An oil spillage can be soaked up by placing litter on the area.

* Fullers' earth is also used in cases of paraquat poisoning. If eaten, it absorbs the poison, which is later eliminated from the body along with the litter.

In the garden

Don't grow catnip (*Nepeta Cataria*) in your garden
unless you love everybody's cats. Because
everybody's cats will congregate there!

If you don't mind attracting other cats to your garden,
catnip can be grown from seed in a pot or outdoors.
Plant in a seed bed in May or June in a sunny position
to transplant later to its flowering position. Catnip is a
perennial which likes chalky soil.

Pick catnip at its peak on a sunny day and dry by
hanging in bunches in a dark, cool place. Or freeze it
in 3-inch pieces in small plastic bags. You can defrost
it as required for a summer treat all winter long.

Cats love to use the fine, freshly turned soil of flower-
beds as lavatories. To protect your prize begonias, give
your cat a large sandbox. Naturally fastidious, a cat
will prefer to use it and you can remove the solid
waste for burying every week. Make sure no children
use the sandbox, however, as intestinal worms can be
transmitted in this way.

There's an old countryman's tip to keep cats off your
flower-bed. Scatter pieces of orange rind on the soil.
Perhaps this works for old countrymen – it doesn't
discourage my cats!

Prevent cats from rolling and digging in seed-beds by
covering the soil with old sheets. Wet them to dis-

courage your cat further. Or stick twigs in rows along your seed drills. Seedlings can be protected in this way too.

To discourage your cat from nibbling your plants, spray them with a mixture of a teaspoon of Tabasco sauce in four pints of water. It'll discourage bugs too!

Cats will enjoy having a natural scratching post – a tree. To protect a particular tree from damage, tie some plastic netting around the lower part of the trunk to discourage scratching.

Cats nibble leaves and grass as an aid to digestion. Read instructions carefully on insecticides and herbicides and don't allow cats out when spraying your garden or for a few days afterwards.

The cat-loving gardener should remember that the following can be toxic to cats: dieffenbachias, poinsettias, chrysanthemums, philodendrons, yew, winter cherry, oleander, Jerusalem cherry, daffodils, crocuses, laurel, azaleas, rhododendrons, larkspur, foxglove, hyacinths, castor oil plants, mistletoe, iris, lupins, laburnum, broom, monkshood and lily-of-the-valley.

If your cat has killed a mouse or bird, don't let the death be in vain. Bury the body by the roots of your perennials where it will nourish the soil. Incidentally, although cats will often kill shrews, they won't eat them. They taste bitter – although I don't speak from personal experience.

Warnings

Catnip can be an excellent training tool, encouraging your cat to use his basket, litter tray or scratching post. However, it works on the cat's nervous system and dulls his senses, so don't allow him outside near traffic, dogs or unsympathetic humans for at least half an hour after using catnip.

A cat's collar should not be too tight. If you can insert one finger between the collar and his neck, it's just right. If you can insert two or three fingers, it's too loose and may get caught on something.

Dispose of anti-freeze carefully. *Ethylene Glycol* is a common anti-freeze ingredient and is poisonous, yet it has a sweet taste which attracts cats (and children and dogs).

Be careful which disinfectants or antiseptics you use on or around cats. Cats are unable to detoxify phenols. Don't use Dettol, TCP or any disinfectant containing chlorinated phenols, all of which will be toxic. Savlon is OK. Jeyes Fluid is also toxic to cats – use a solution of Domestos and water instead.

Never be tempted to give aspirin or paracetemol to a cat in pain. It could kill him. Call your vet instead of trying to treat him yourself.

Always be careful when closing doors. You could break your cat's back if you shut the door on him.

Don't allow your cat to play with string or yarn when you're not around to hold the other end of it. Cats have rasp-like tongues and, once string gets into their mouths, it's easier to swallow it than to spit it out. The string can end up knotting the intestines and major surgery may be needed to remove it.

Paper and balls of foil should only be allowed as playthings under close supervision. Anything small enough to swallow is totally unsuitable as a plaything.

Remember, never use a flea spray on your cat within several days of worming him. Used together, the two treatments can be toxic. And don't use a flea spray on very young kittens. Ask your vet to recommend a suitable flea treatment. You should also ask your vet's advice about worming very young kittens, as an overdose could prove fatal.

Tail-pieces

Don't feed your cat for four hours prior to travelling —
many cats are bad travellers. If he really hates
travelling and a journey is necessary, see your vet. He
may prescribe a mild sedative to make the journey
easier for your cat.

Sprinkle a little catnip in your cat's carrying basket. It
can make a journey more enjoyable.

Cats will sleep about 16 hours a day but may want to
play while *you* sleep. Don't forget that training will
minimise this; a firm, loud 'no' will often get the
message across. If it doesn't, try saying 'no' followed
by a well-aimed cushion!

Cats will sleep better after a good meal, so you could
try changing their meal-times. Give the main meal an
hour or so before you go to bed and your cat will
spend the remainder of the night sleeping it off.

If your cat persists in behaving badly, make a loud
noise that sounds like 'pssst!' To a cat, it sounds like
another cat hissing and it will stop him in his tracks.

Or stop him from doing something he shouldn't by
blowing at him. Or squirt him with air from a bicycle
pump. Cats hate it!

If your cat presents you with a dead mouse or bird,
don't shriek in terror or shout at him. He is bringing

you a gift — his contribution to your social group's food store. Thank him and ask him to take the offering outside. He'll usually be happy to take it away — he was only offering it to you out of politeness anyway.

A cat is simply following his natural instincts when he hunts prey but, if this upsets you, put a bell on his collar. Take it off when he's indoors or all that dinging will drive him (and you) crazy.

If your cat persists in chasing birds and you're a bird-lover as well as a cat-lover, make a 'bird' for him from a bundle of feathers tied to a long string. Dangle the feathers in front of him and have a water-pistol handy. When he attacks the feathers, let him have a squirt of water. He'll soon learn that feathers = water and he won't realise that you're the one dowsing him.

If your cat catches a live mouse or bird which you want to rescue and he won't give it up, distract his attention. Throw down a hanky a few feet from him or trail a piece of string for him to chase. With luck, he'll drop his prey, leaving it to run away.

'Lost' cats are often just trapped — locked in an out-house or shed nearby. If you learn the boundaries of your cat's territory, you'll know where to start look-ing. Start your search in the closed sheds within his area. Spayed females will usually have a territory which consists of your garden and the one next door. Neutered toms will have a territory about three times as large, while unneutered cats can have a territory which stretches two to three miles.

Catnip is a great aid to relaxing a nervous cat if the cat is susceptible to it. Some cats aren't. In their case, try giving them some melon or stoned olives. It has the same effect on some cats!

Don't allow your cat to play constantly with catnip toys. They should be kept in an airtight container to prolong their effect and taken out occasionally for five or ten minutes' play.

A golf practice ball – the sort with holes cut into it – makes an inexpensive, safe toy. It's lightweight and your cat will be able to toss it about. He may enjoy batting it around in the bath – but be sure to empty the water out first!

Cats make wonderful companions for the elderly or infirm, because of their independence. However, there could be serious consequences if the owner tripped over the cat. If a cat is to live in such a household, try to accustom him from kittenhood to getting out of the way. If he won't, the elderly or infirm owner should always shuffle, rather than walk, around the home. Their foot may connect with the cat but they shouldn't fall over him.

Remember to take your cat's personal preferences into account when buying a cat bed. If he likes to sleep stretched out, he'll need a bigger bed than a cat which sleeps curled up. Assertive cats may not like a hooded bed which means that they don't have a clear field of view. And no cat will like sleeping in a high traffic area, or too near his litter box. If he simply *won't* use his bed, try placing it high up, on a stable piece of furniture. In the wild, a cat will often choose to sleep high up – he feels more secure that way.

If your cat fidgets and won't settle in a room with you, buy him a comfortable bed or beanbag and place it in a warm, draught-free spot in the room. You may then have trouble prising him out of it.

Remember, in your cat's social group, you are considered to be the senior cat and group leader. You acquire that status when you expect your cat to live by your rules. This gives you certain responsibilities; as chief food provider, for instance. You are also expected to take your cat's side in an argument when a strange cat enters your territory, by chasing it away.

You'll find that chasing strange cats confers great status upon you in your cat's eyes and he will be reinforced in the belief that he has chosen the right group leader!

Most important of all, make friends with your cat. Talk to him and explain things to him, especially if major changes in your lifestyle are on the way. Form a mental picture of whatever you're explaining and you'll be astounded at how much he will understand, whether it be from your words or from your mental picture. Cats understand much more than we will ever know.

Useful addresses

Charities
Cats Protection League, 17 King's Road, Horsham, West Sussex RH13 5PP.
Feline Advisory Bureau, 350 Upper Richmond Road, London SW15 6TL.
People's Dispensary for Sick Animals, PDSA House, South Street, Dorking, Surrey RH4 2LB.
Royal Society for the Prevention of Cruelty to Animals, The Causeway, Horsham, West Sussex RH12 1HQ.

Litter
If you have difficulty finding a stockist of Fullers' earth near you, contact:
Laporte Industries, Nutfield Road, Redhill, Surrey RH1 4EE.

Magazine
Cat World, Scan House, Southwick Street, Southwick, Brighton, BN4 4TE. £1 monthly.

Registration Organisations (both hold cat shows)
The Cat Association, CA Central Office, Hunting Grove, Lowfield Heath, Crawley, West Sussex. Formed 1983.
The Governing Council of the Cat Fancy, 4–6 Penel Orlieu, Bridgwater, Somerset. Formed 1910.

Seedsmen
Thompson and Morgan, London Road, Ipswich, Suffolk.